Weekly Reader Books presents

Heroes of the Revolution

John Hancock

By Susan & John Lee

Illustrated by Chuck Mitchell

 CHILDRENS PRESS, CHICAGO

This book is a presentation of Weekly Reader Books.
Weekly Reader Books offers book clubs for children from
preschool to young adulthood.

For further information write to:
Weekly Reader Books
1250 Fairwood Ave.
Columbus, Ohio 43216

Library of Congress Cataloging in Publication Data

Lee, Susan.
  John Hancock.

  (Heroes of the Revolution)
  SUMMARY: An easy-to-read biography of the man whose
prominent signature on the Declaration of Independence
was indicative of his dedication to the revolutionary
cause.
  1. Hancock, John, 1737-1793. [1. Hancock, John,
1737-1793. 2. United States — History — Revolution —
Biography] I. Lee, John, joint author. II. Mitchell,
Chuck, illus. III. Title.
E302.6.H23L43   973.3'092'4 [B]   [92]   73-19971
ISBN 0-516-04653-5

One of the first things you learn in school is how to write your name. You write your name in your books. You write it on your school papers. Why does your teacher need your name on your school work? Do you write letters? Don't you sign your name at the end of each letter? What other times do you have to know how to write your name?

In America when you write your name many people say this is your "John Hancock." You write your "John Hancock" by writing your name. This is the story of why writing a "John Hancock" means writing a name. It is a story that begins many years ago, more than two hundred years ago.

4

In 1737 a son was born to John and Mary Hancock. They named their first child John. The Hancock family lived in a small town near the city of Boston. In those days the English King ruled the country you live in now. There was no United States of America. The people did not live in states. They lived in one of the English colonies along the Atlantic Ocean.

John Hancock and his mother and father lived in the colony of Massachusetts. They were English colonists. They lived under English law, and called England their "mother country."

When John was a young boy, his father
died. Mrs. Hancock was very poor. She
had three children to feed. It was hard to
make ends meet. She asked John's uncle to
help her.

John's uncle, Thomas Hancock, was a
rich man. He had many ships. These ships
sailed from Massachusetts to London.
They went back and forth with goods to
sell. Uncle Thomas got rich from the
things he sold.

John's aunt and uncle wanted to help.
They asked John, the oldest child, to live
with them in Boston. Uncle Thomas and
Aunt Lydia had no children. They were
very happy when John came to live with
them.

John Hancock was a lucky boy. He had
a rich uncle to take care of him. Uncle
Thomas sent John to the best schools. John
had fine clothes to wear.

When John was out of school, he went on a trip. He sailed for London. He made many new friends. He even met the English King. He spent a lot of money. In one letter he wrote, "I find money some way or other goes very fast."

When John came back from England, he went to work for his uncle. In 1764 Thomas Hancock died. He left all his ships to John. John was one of the richest men in the colony of Massachusetts. He was only 27 years old!

At first John did well. His ships sailed across the Atlantic Ocean with goods for the people of London. His ships sailed back with goods to sell the colonists. Many colonists needed and bought the goods made in England, the mother country.

John Hancock made a lot of money. He was generous, too. He gave food and firewood to the poor in the winter. He also gave a lot of money to the churches of Boston. Many people liked John Hancock because he was a kind man.

Then trouble began. In 1767 the English made new laws. The laws made the colonists pay new taxes. Men with ships had even more taxes to pay. John Hancock had to pay taxes on many of the goods he sold.

John Hancock did not want to obey these new laws. He said the laws were not fair because none of the colonists had helped to make the laws. Sometimes he took his goods into Boston at night when the English were not looking. In that way he got out of paying taxes.

One day in May of 1768, a Hancock ship called the *Liberty* sailed into Boston with a cargo of wine. That night, men working for John Hancock took the wine off the *Liberty*. They did not pay the tax man any taxes on the wine.

A tax man saw Hancock's men take the wine ashore. He told the English what John Hancock had done. The English had heard stories about Hancock. He had not paid taxes before. They decided to teach John Hancock a lesson.

John Hancock did not know what the English had learned. He kept on with his work, and had his sailors load new goods on the *Liberty*. By June 10 it was ready to leave Boston.

But the *Liberty* was never put to sea.
Instead, men from an English warship
boarded Hancock's ship. An official of the
King nailed a paper to the ship. It said that
the *Liberty* was no longer John Hancock's.
John Hancock could not keep his boat
because he had not paid taxes on the cargo
of wine.

Then some sailors began to sail the *Liberty* over to the English warship. As they sailed away, an angry mob on shore threw rocks and bricks at the sailors. They did not want the English to take John Hancock's ship away from him.

It was not long before John Hancock
learned what the English had done. He
wanted to get his ship back, but he would
not pay any taxes to do it. The tax collector
could not prove that John had gotten out of
paying taxes on that night, but the English
kept his ship just the same.

Soon, everyone in Boston was talking
about John Hancock. Here was a man who
would rather lose his ship than pay the new
taxes. He was not afraid to stand up for his
rights, even if the cost was high.

The story of the *Liberty* got the people of
Boston talking about the taxes. They had
not helped make the tax law. Why should
they have to pay taxes? Many people
stopped buying English goods to show the
King how mad they were.

People in all the colonies began to write letters. They wrote to the men in London who made the laws. They asked for a change in the laws. Finally the English took all the taxes away but one. They left the tax on tea.

John Hancock was still not happy. He did not like the tea tax. His friends did not like the tax. One of his best friends was Sam Adams.

John Hancock and Sam Adams began to talk against the English. They said that England was taking their freedom away. In time, everyone in Boston knew that John and Sam did not like the English. They called John Hancock, Sam Adams, and their friends the "Sons of Liberty."

The Sons of Liberty asked the people of Boston not to buy English tea. They put signs up in the street. They told the English to take their ships and their tea back to London. But the English would not sail back to London.

The Sons of Liberty had a plan. One cold December night in 1773, they dressed up as Indians. They went down to Boston's harbor and got on the English ships. Then they threw all the tea into the water. Soon the people of Boston were singing:

"Rally Indians! Bring out your axes,
And tell King George we'll pay no taxes."

The colonists knew who planned the "Boston Tea Party." It was John Hancock and Sam Adams. The English knew too. They did not like these two trouble-makers.

King George was very mad when he
learned about the Boston Tea Party.
Ships of war sailed from London. Soon,
English soldiers came to Boston. John
Hancock and his friend Sam Adams were
in danger!

The people of Boston did not want
English soldiers in their town. They
wanted the soldiers to go home. They
called them "Redcoats" and other names.
Life was not very happy for the soldiers.

In the small towns near Boston, many men got ready to fight the English Redcoats. These colonists were called Minute Men because they could get ready to fight in less than a minute. The Minute Men hid their guns so the English soldiers would not find them.

The Sons of Liberty watched the soldiers all the time. They wanted to learn England's plans. If the soldiers made a move, the Sons of Liberty knew what it was.

At last, the English general had a plan. He decided to send his men on a raid. They were to look for hidden guns in the small towns near Boston. He told the soldiers to take the guns away from the colonial Minute Men.

The general also asked his men to find John Hancock and Sam Adams. These two men had talked against the King. What troublemakers! They would be sent to London to be tried. If they were found guilty, they might even be hung!

On April 18, 1775, the soldiers began to leave Boston by night. But the Sons of Liberty were watching. Paul Revere, one of the Sons of Liberty, rode off to warn the Minute Men and find John Hancock and Sam Adams.

Paul Revere rode his horse as fast as it would go. He found John Hancock and Sam Adams in Lexington, Massachusetts. He told them they were in danger. Then Paul Revere got back on his horse and rode off to warn the Minute Men that the British were coming.

John Hancock and his friend talked all
night long. Hancock wanted to stay and
fight the English. But Sam Adams said they
must get away. Sam wanted them to be free
to lead the colonists. At last John said yes.

Suddenly the two men heard gunfire.
The Minute Men and English soldiers
were shooting at each other! The colonists
would not give up their guns without a
fight.

John Hancock and Sam Adams ran into
the woods. The soldiers were close behind.
But John Hancock knew these woods better
than the English. The soldiers looked all
over, but the two leaders got away safely.

A few days after the fight at Lexington,
John Hancock and Sam Adams left
Massachusetts. News of the fight went with
them. People in other colonies had heard
about the brave Minute Men and their
fight with the English. They waved and
cheered as John Hancock rode by.

Liberty Hall

John Hancock and other leaders went to Philadelphia for a meeting, called a Congress. Leading men from all thirteen colonies were there. Each had been chosen by the people of their colony to speak for them. Philadelphia was a good meeting place because it was the largest city in all the colonies.

These men had a lot of work to do. They chose John Hancock as President of the Congress. Most of the colonists did not want to go to war because of the fighting in Massachusetts. So they wrote King George and tried to make up. But they also voted and made George Washington the general of the colonial army.

When King George heard about the Congress, he was very mad. He wanted the Congress to stop, and the men to go home. He did not want to make up. He wanted the colonists to obey his laws.

More colonists began to talk about being
free of England, the mother country. They
felt like Americans, not English colonists.
Some people were afraid of the English
army. But many others wanted
independence and were not afraid to fight
the Redcoats.

The men in Philadelphia did not obey King George. The Congress went on. The men talked about independence. John Hancock wanted independence. He wanted all the colonies to vote for independence. But some men were not sure.

On July 2, 1776, John Hancock began the meeting. This was the day that the men from all thirteen colonies were going to vote on independence. Would they vote to be free of England? Twelve colonies voted yes! Only the colony of New York did not vote for independence.

Two days later, on July 4, 1776, the men voted again. This time, they voted on a Declaration of Independence. It was written by Thomas Jefferson.

The Declaration of Independence said why the colonies wanted to be free of England. It said that King George had taxed the colonists unfairly. It said the King was taking their freedoms away. Again, all the colonies voted yes to the declaration but New York.

On August 2, 1776, the men met again to sign the Declaration of Independence. President John Hancock was the first man to sign. He signed his name in very large letters.

There is a story about what John Hancock said when he signed the Declaration of Independence. He said he wrote his name large so that the King would not need his glasses to read it. He wanted to be sure King George saw his name.

No one knows if Hancock really said
this. But every man at the Congress knew
John Hancock was brave. He wanted
independence, and he was not afraid to say
so. If the English got him, John Hancock
would lose his money, his ships, and his
life.

The English never got John Hancock.
When the war was over, and the
Americans had won independence, John
Hancock was safe. He wanted to help his
new state get started.

The people of Massachusetts loved John Hancock because he had not been afraid of the King. They chose him as their first governor. He was still governor of Massachusetts when he died in 1793.

Americans still remember the good name of John Hancock. He spoke without fear. He put his life in danger for freedom. He wrote his name on the Declaration of Independence so the King would see it. Today, if you look at the Declaration, you will see a large . . .

John Hancock

About the Authors:

Susan Dye Lee has been writing professionally since she graduated from college in 1961. Working with the Social Studies Curriculum Center at Northwestern University, she has created course materials in American studies. Ms. Lee has also co-authored a text on Latin America and Canada, written case studies in legal history for the Law in American Society Project, and developed a teacher's guide for tapes that explore woman's role in America's past. The writer credits her students for many of her ideas. Currently, she is doing research for her history dissertation on the Women's Christian Temperance Union for Northwestern University. In her free moments, Susan Lee enjoys traveling, playing the piano, and welcoming friends to "Highland Cove," the summer cottage she and her husband, John, share.

John R. Lee enjoys a prolific career as a writer, teacher, and outdoorsman. After receiving his doctorate in social studies at Stanford, Dr. Lee came to Northwestern University's School of Education, where he advises student teachers and directs graduates in training. A versatile writer, Dr. Lee has co-authored the Scott-Foresman social studies textbooks for primary-age children. In addition, he has worked on the production of 50 films and over 100 filmstrips. His biographical film on Helen Keller received a 1970 Venice Film Festival award. His college text, *Teaching Social Studies in the Elementary School,* has recently been published. Besides pro-football, John Lee's passion is his Wisconsin cottage, where he likes to shingle leaky roofs, split wood, and go sailing.

About the Artist

Chuck Mitchell is a Chicago artist who specializes in editorial and book illustration.